SAYINGS and PHRASES

You're Clean as a Whistle!

(And Other Silly Sayings)

SOAP

written by Cynthia Klingel ★ *illustrated by Mernie Gallagher-Cole*

ABOUT THE AUTHOR

As a high school English teacher and as an elementary teacher, Cynthia Klingel has shared her love of language with students. She has always been fascinated with idioms and figures of speech. Today Cynthia is a school district administrator in Minnesota. She has two daughters who also share her love of language through reading, writing, and talking!

ABOUT THE ILLUSTRATOR

Mernie Gallagher-Cole lives in Pennsylvania with her husband and two children. She uses sayings and phrases like the ones in this book every day. She has illustrated many children's books, including *Messy Molly* and *Día De Los Muertos* for The Child's World®.

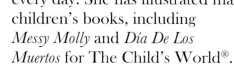

The Child's World®

Published in the United States of America
by The Child's World®
1980 Lookout Drive • Mankato, MN 56003-1705
800-599-READ • www.childsworld.com

ACKNOWLEDGMENTS
The Child's World®: Mary Berendes, Publishing Director

The Creative Spark: Editing

The Design Lab: Kathleen Petelinsek, Design and Page Production

LIBRARY OF CONGRESS CATALOGING-IN-PUBLICATION DATA
Klingel, Cynthia Fitterer.
You're clean as a whistle!: (and other silly sayings) / by Cynthia Klingel.
    p. cm.—(Sayings and phrases)
 ISBN-13: 978-1-59296-905-0 (lib. bdg.: alk. paper)
 ISBN-10: 1-59296-905-4 (lib. bdg.: alk. paper)
1. English language—Idioms—Juvenile literature.
2. Figures of speech—Juvenile literature. I. Title.
II. Series.
PE1460.K686 2007
428—dc22   2007004216

People use idioms (ID-ee-umz) every day. These are sayings and phrases with meanings that are different from the actual words. Some idioms seem silly. Many of them don't make much sense . . . at first.

This book will help you understand some of the most common idioms. It will tell you how you might hear a saying or phrase. It will tell you what the saying really means. All of these sayings and short phrases—even the silly ones—are an important part of our language!

TABLE *of* CONTENTS

Ace in the hole	4
The apple of my eye	4
Barking up the wrong tree	5
Between a rock and a hard place	6
Bright-eyed and bushy-tailed	7
By the skin of your teeth	8
Called on the carpet	8
Clean as a whistle	9
Crocodile tears	9
A dime a dozen	10
Draw the line	10
Dressed to the nines	11
Have cold feet	12
If the shoe fits, wear it	12
Jump ship	13
Kill two birds with one stone	13
Let your hair down	14
Make a mountain out of a molehill	14
Mind your Ps and Qs	15
Monkey business	15
Off the deep end	16
Out of sight, out of mind	16
Paint the town red	17
A picture paints a thousand words	17
A pig in a poke	18
Pull up stakes	18
Put the cart before the horse	19
Read between the lines	20
Selling like hotcakes	21
Smell like a rose	21
Stuffed shirt	22
Turn the other cheek	23
Wet behind the ears	23
A wolf in sheep's clothing	24

Ace in the hole

The big baseball game was on Saturday. The Tigers were sure they would beat the Mustangs. But what the Tigers didn't know is that a home run hitter had just returned to the Mustang team. He would be the Mustangs' ace in the hole.

MEANING: To have something valuable that is kept secret until it is used

The apple of my eye

Dana was going to visit her grandma. Her grandma loved Dana's visits. They did many things together. They always had fun. Dana knew her grandma was very proud of her. Her grandma liked to tell her, "Dana, you are the apple of my eye!"

MEANING: Something that means a lot to you or that is important to you

Barking up the wrong tree

Maria came back to the kitchen to find her snack half eaten. That little brother of hers! Suddenly her brother's friend Ricky came around the corner. He was eating Maria's snack! She had been barking up the wrong tree. It wasn't her brother who ate her snack after all!

MEANING: To make a mistake about another person; to focus on the wrong thing or have the wrong idea about something

Between a rock and a hard place

Brent's football team was in the championship game on Friday. The team had an important practice Thursday night. Brent's brother Ben was in his first soccer game on Thursday night. It was important for Brent to be there to watch Ben. But his football teammates needed him to be at practice. What should he do? Either way Brent would be making someone unhappy. He was between a rock and a hard place.

MEANING: To have to make a difficult decision; to have choices, but none that are good

Bright-eyed and bushy-tailed

"Time to get up! Time to get up!" squealed Nicky. "Santa came. Let's open presents!"

Mom rolled over and looked at the clock. It was only 6:00!

"Nicky, it's so early. You sure are bright-eyed and bushy-tailed for this time of day," answered Mom.

MEANING: To be wide awake and full of energy

By the skin of your teeth

Every day, Mark walked by the same house on his way home from school. The house's yard had a fence, and inside was a barking dog. The dog looked very mean. Mark knew he was safe because the dog couldn't get through the fence.

One day Mark saw that the gate was open. The dog saw Mark and began running toward him. Mark grabbed the gate and shut it—just as the dog leaped toward him! That was a close call. Mark had escaped by the skin of his teeth!

MEANING: To have a narrow escape; to barely miss something

Called on the carpet

Gina was in trouble. This was the third time she had faked her way through a book report. Her teacher, Mr. Tran, knew Gina was not reading the assignments. Now Gina was to meet with him after class. He was going to call her on the carpet. She just knew it.

MEANING: For a parent or other person in charge to scold someone for doing something wrong

Clean as a whistle

Zach was in the kitchen when he heard someone crying at the back door. It was his little brother, Tim.

"What's the matter, buddy?" Zach asked.

Tim rubbed his eyes. " I dropped my new car in the mud," he said. "Now it's ruined!"

Zach took the toy car over to the kitchen sink. He ran it under the water, dried it off, and handed it back. "Here you go," he said. "Clean as a whistle!"

MEANING: To be completely clean

Crocodile tears

Ava wanted to go to the sleepover. Her mom said no. Her dad said no. Ava begged and pleaded. She whined. She promised to clean her room. She promised to walk the dog. Her parents still said no. Ava decided she would cry to make her parents feel sorry for her.

"Ava, stop crying those crocodile tears," said Dad. "No means no."

MEANING: To pretend to be sad

A dime a dozen

Mom was having a garage sale. Pedro was excited because he thought of a way to make some money.

"Hey, Mom," said Pedro. "Remember all of those extra baseball cards I have? Do you think I could sell them at the garage sale?"

"You can try, Pedro," answered Mom. "But those extras you have are pretty common. I'm not sure anyone else wants them, either. They're a dime a dozen if you ask me."

MEANING: Something that is not worth much because it is common and easy to get

Draw the line

Ella was planning her birthday party. It started out with plans for three friends coming over after school. Then she thought they could go bowling. Ella decided to add two more friends. Now there would be five guests. Ella remembered that everyone would be hungry. Mom agreed they could go out for pizza after bowling. Now Ella could think of four more people she wanted to invite. Ella asked Mom.

"That's it, Ella," answered Mom. "This is where I draw the line. No more guests and no more party changes."

MEANING: Someone has reached his or her limit

Dressed to the nines

It was Ramona's birthday. Her family was going to a nice restaurant and then to a play to celebrate. She had a beautiful new dress with new shoes that sparkled. She fixed her hair up with shiny ribbons. Now she just wished everyone else would hurry up!

Finally she heard them coming downstairs.

"Oh, my!" exclaimed Dad when he saw Ramona. "You look so fancy! You certainly are dressed to the nines tonight!"

MEANING: To be very dressed up; to wear fancy clothes and look nice

Have cold feet

Kate really wanted to be class president. The election was next week. But first she had to give a big speech to the whole school. That really scared her. She was having second thoughts. Maybe she didn't want to do this after all.

"You've wanted to be class president for a long time," said Mom. "You're not getting cold feet, are you?"

MEANING: To suddenly decide not to do something; to stop something you've already started

If the shoe fits, wear it

The boys were relaxing on the porch when Mom walked through.

"I just spent the last twenty minutes cleaning up the toys in the den," said Mom. "I wish whoever used them would have put them away."

"It wasn't me!" exclaimed Troy.

"I'm not blaming anyone," explained Mom. "But if the shoe fits, wear it."

MEANING: If you did something, accept responsibility for it. If someone makes a comment that refers to you, admit that the comment is about you.

Jump ship

Dad was planning a family trip for the weekend. Travis thought it was going to be very boring. He did not want to go. In fact, it was the last thing he wanted to do.

"Hey, Dad," said Travis. "I'd like to stay home with Grandma instead of going this weekend. Is that OK?"

"What?" replied Dad. "You mean you're going to jump ship? I guess that would be all right."

MEANING: To decide not to do something or be involved in something

Kill two birds with one stone

"Mom!" called Leslie. "Where are you? I need to go to the mall. I have to buy a present for the party tonight."

"Mom can't take you now," said Leslie's brother, Scott. "She has to take me to the sports shop. I have to go get a new hockey stick. Practice starts in two days."

"Tell you what," said Mom. "How about if we all go together? I'll drop Leslie at the mall. It's right by the sports shop. She can get the present while we get your hockey stick. That way we'll kill two birds with one stone."

MEANING: To save time or effort by doing two things at once

Let your hair down

Mom had been very busy at work all week. She had not had any time for fun.

"I'm home!" exclaimed Mom on Friday afternoon.

"Mom, can we do something fun this weekend?" asked Jennifer.

"Fun sounds good," replied Mom. "I'm done with my big project. I'm ready to let my hair down and have a great weekend!"

MEANING: To relax and just be yourself

Make a mountain out of a molehill

Kevin was tired of his sister's whining. She always had to have everything her way. Now she was trying to tell their parents that Kevin had embarrassed her at school. It was so untrue!

"Megan," said their mom. "Kevin probably shouldn't have said what he did, but I think you're making a mountain out of a molehill."

MEANING: To turn something little into something much bigger; to exaggerate

Mind your Ps and Qs

Grace's dad was a teacher. Ms. Moss was the principal there. Grace had never met her. One day, she went to school with her father.

"Mind your Ps and Qs if we see Ms. Moss," said her father. "I've told her so many nice things about you!"

MEANING: To do things right; to be very careful and pay attention

Monkey business

Alex was bored. He was tired of working quietly at his desk. It was time to make some people laugh! He leaned over and told Nathan what he was going to do.

"Alex! Your monkey business is going to get you in trouble!" warned Nathan.

MEANING: To be silly; to get in trouble

Off the deep end

The soccer game had not gone well. In fact, the whole season had not been a good one. Coach was fed up. After the game, he talked to the team. He got angrier and angrier. Soon he was yelling. His face got red and he threw his hat on the ground. Finally he stormed off the field.

Sam turned to his teammate, Robbie.

"I know we didn't do very well today," whispered Sam. "But Coach sure was mad! He was acting a little crazy. I think Coach has gone off the deep end!"

MEANING: To act in a way that seems out of control

Out of sight, out of mind

Tanner had taken the clock apart and now his dad wanted him to put it together. He would do it later, after skateboarding. Dad said that would be okay. Tanner went to put it in the closet.

"Wait a minute," said Dad. "Why don't you leave all those pieces right here on the table. That way when you come home you'll remember to do it. If you put it in the closet, you might not remember. Out of sight, out of mind."

MEANING: If something is hidden or not in plain view, it is easy to forget about it.

Paint the town red

Tonight had been the championship basketball game. Keith's team had won! Now the whole team was ready to have fun and celebrate. Keith was ready to go.

"Come on, everyone!" yelled Keith. "Let's go! I'm ready to paint the town red!"

MEANING: To celebrate or have a good time

A picture paints a thousand words

Josie's mother was trying to describe the new house they had just bought.

"I don't get it, Mom," said Josie.

"Here," said her mom. She handed Josie a stack of photos. "A picture paints a thousand words."

MEANING: Some things just can't be explained very well with words. Seeing a picture often makes it very clear.

A pig in a poke

Linda was excited. Her friend had just sold her some used video games. Linda didn't think she paid too much for them. Now she was trying the first one. It didn't work. The second one didn't work. Linda couldn't believe it. Her mom helped her try the third one. It didn't work, either.

"I don't know Linda," sighed Mom. "I think you bought a pig in a poke."

MEANING: To buy or get something that has less value than you thought it would have

Pull up stakes

Every fall Tony's family picked apples at Johnson's Apple Farm. The Johnsons had become friends of Tony's family. This year Tony noticed a "For Sale" sign in the yard.

"What does this sign mean?" Tony asked Mr. Johnson.

"We're getting older," sighed Mr. Johnson. "The farm takes a lot of work. Mrs. Johnson and I decided it was time to pull up stakes. We're moving to a smaller house in town."

MEANING: To move from where you're living. Often, the move is to a better place or for a better life.

Put the cart before the horse

Sadie wanted new skis for her birthday. She had been talking about them for months. Now she had more ideas.

"Mom, I have some more ideas for my birthday," declared Sadie. "I'll need a ski pass. I'll need a new ski coat to match my skis, too."

"Stop, Sadie," warned Mom. "You don't even have the skis yet. You're putting the cart before the horse."

MEANING: To do something out of order; to do something that should come later instead of doing the things that come first

Read between the lines

Darrin had gotten in big trouble at school. He was even called to the principal's office. The principal sent a note home to Darrin's mother. Darrin read the note. He didn't think it sounded all that bad! He had thought it would be a lot worse.

His mother read the note when Darrin got home.

"Do you realize how serious this is?" asked his mother. "Your principal is very upset with you, and I am too!"

"But his note wasn't that bad. Mr. Morales didn't say he was really upset. The note didn't sound that serious to me."

"Darrin," responded his mother. "I can read between the lines. You are in big trouble here."

MEANING: To understand what someone is thinking or trying to say, even though he or she did not say it that way

Selling like hotcakes

Cindy and Taylor were having a cookie stand in the front yard. Mom didn't think they'd sell many, but they were doing it anyway. Suddenly Cindy burst into the kitchen.

"Quick, Mom!" she exclaimed. "Please make another batch. In fact, make two more batches. Our cookies are selling like hotcakes!"

MEANING: To be very popular or to sell very quickly

Smell like a rose

Evan was tired. He had dropped a bowl of salad all over the kitchen floor. Dressing spilled onto the cupboards. Lettuce and vegetables had scattered everywhere. Evan washed the cupboards and scrubbed the floor. He made a new salad. Finally everything was ready for supper.

"Look at this kitchen," said Dad with a whistle. "Your mother is going to be surprised at how clean everything is! And the salad looks delicious."

"Will Mom be mad about the bowl I broke?" asked Evan.

"Oh, I don't think so," said Dad with a smile. "In fact, I'd say you'll probably come out of this smelling like a rose."

MEANING: To end up in a good position

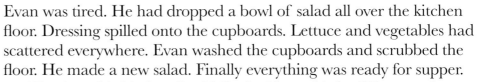

Stuffed shirt

Donna loved spending time with her relatives. They were so much fun! Except for Uncle Sal. He never played with Donna or her cousins. He only talked with the adults. He never laughed at jokes. In fact, sometimes he even acted as if he didn't like jokes at all! One day Donna heard her mom and dad talking about Uncle Sal.

"I don't understand Sal," said her mother. "He was so fun when he was younger. Now he's turned into a stuffed shirt."

MEANING: Someone who doesn't seem to have a sense of humor or who doesn't join people in doing fun things. Often people acting this way seem to think they are better than other people.

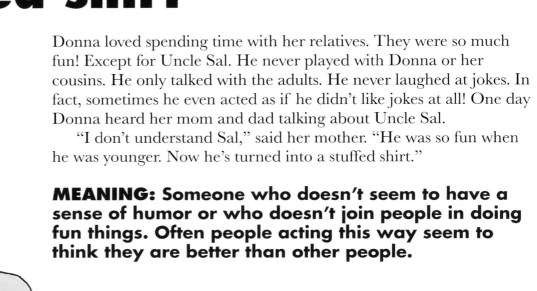

Turn the other cheek

"I'm so mad at Rachel!" cried Kara. "She lied about me to our teacher."

"Does your teacher know that?" asked Dad.

"Yes. Rachel had to apologize. We're supposed to make up," explained Kara.

"Good. Then I suggest you turn the other cheek and move on," answered Dad.

MEANING: To forgive someone who has done something wrong to you; to ignore something unkind that's been done to you

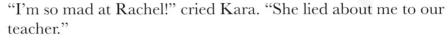

Wet behind the ears

Lola was very excited. The neighbors had just had a new baby. Lola was in fourth grade and was excited to start babysitting. But the neighbors hadn't called yet.

"Mom, do you think the neighbors will call me to babysit?" asked Lola.

"Honey, I think they might need someone a little older. You're pretty wet behind the ears when it comes to babysitting a brand new baby."

MEANING: To be young or without a lot of experience

A wolf in sheep's clothing

Tad was confused. Derek had always been a bully. Suddenly, Derek was being nice. He wanted to be best friends. He wanted to do homework together. He wanted Tad to hang out on the playground. Tad thought it might be all right to invite Derek over to play checkers.

"I don't know, Tad," answered Dad. "You've talked about Derek many times before. You've told me how he's upset you. I'm not sure if I trust him, yet. He could be a wolf in sheep's clothing."

MEANING: A person who seems nice and harmless, but really isn't; a person who is being nice because they are trying to fool you or get you to do something